Powerful Lessons From Someone Who Has Gone Bankrupt

Your Guide to Investing in a Business with Guaranteed Success

By: Wendy Turner

9781635014303

I0500300

PUBLISHERS NOTES

Disclaimer – Speedy Publishing LLC

This publication is intended to provide helpful and informative material. It is not intended to diagnose, treat, cure, or prevent any health problem or condition, nor is intended to replace the advice of a physician. No action should be taken solely on the contents of this book. Always consult your physician or qualified health-care professional on any matters regarding your health and before adopting any suggestions in this book or drawing inferences from it.

The author and publisher specifically disclaim all responsibility for any liability, loss or risk, personal or otherwise, which is incurred as a consequence, directly or indirectly, from the use or application of any contents of this book.

Any and all product names referenced within this book are the trademarks of their respective owners. None of these owners have sponsored, authorized, endorsed, or approved this book.

Always read all information provided by the manufacturers' product labels before using their products. The author and publisher are not responsible for claims made by manufacturers.

This book was originally printed before 2014. This is an adapted reprint by Speedy Publishing LLC with newly updated content designed to help readers with much more accurate and timely information and data.

Speedy Publishing LLC

40 E Main Street, Newark, Delaware, 19711

Contact Us: 1-888-248-4521

Website: http://www.speedypublishing.co

REPRINTED Paperback Edition: 9781635014303:

Manufactured in the United States of America

DEDICATION

This book is dedicated to Jeff. Thank you for preparing my meals and taking care of the dogs while I was busy writing this book. I owe you this success.

TABLE OF CONTENTS

CHAPTER 1- THE TRUTH BEHIND BANKRUPTCY AND HOW IT AFFECTS YOU

When you are forced to declare yourself bankrupt it is one way of dealing with debts you can no longer manage. But it is not a decision that should be taken lightly.

Bankruptcy is a serious matter that will affect the way you are dealt with by the creditors you wish to establish a relationship for many years after you've been discharged. Bankruptcy is not a fun thing to do or an easy out for those who are buried in debt. It is a way to help those who simply can't see a way out of debt and who don't have the means to pay their debts to get the help that they need. Basically how it works is that you declare yourself bankrupt and the government covers your debt and you are rendered to creditors as 'broke'. This inevitably means that your record will show that you couldn't pay your debts. This makes it very hard for creditors to trust you.

The bankruptcy laws changed in April 2004, and these changes made it easier for people to declare themselves bankrupt by reducing the time it takes to get rid of bankruptcy from three years to one year or less. This change was meant to assist people in getting back on their feet again. For private individuals; which are those that are not running businesses, the effects of personal bankruptcy can be far harder to deal with.

Advantages and Disadvantages of Bankruptcy

The fact is that you shouldn't become bankrupt just because you're struggling with debts. Like I said before, this should only be used as your last resort. The reason for this is because you may be required to give up most of your belongings as a result of it. Some of these might include; salary and any investment in your house. If you own any property or shares in businesses these may have to be sold to pay back the money you owe as well. This means that you could lose your family's house should you decide to go bankrupt.

Even if it is jointly owned by you and a spouse or parent, you may be forced to sell it so your share of the proceeds can be used to repay debts. I will say though that under new rules, if the trustee that is appointed by the court has not sold the bankrupt's home within three years, it no longer counts as part of the estate and may not be reclaimed by you. I wouldn't hold my breath though. This isn't all you could lose either.

If you come into any money while the bankruptcy order is still in place, this could also be taken away from you. This money could come from the lottery, or an inheritance. Of course, you could also find yourself credit blacklisted for up to 15 years. So you should really think before filing for bankruptcy. Bankruptcy is best for someone with considerable debts, no income and no assets.

The people it has the highest effect on are those that actually have equity in property, disposable income and people that have professional qualifications because they stand to lose the most. For example, a lawyer should try to avoid it because they won't be able to practice law once they have filed for bankruptcy.

Perhaps You Don't Need to File for Bankruptcy?

You could write to your creditors and seek an informal arrangement that allows you to pay back your debts over a specific time that they agree on. The only disadvantage to doing this is that it won't be legally binding and your creditor might choose to ignore it later on and seek direct payment. If your debts are relatively small like $5000 or less and you have a regular income the court may agree to set up an order so that you can pay your creditors each month but through the court.

Of course, for debts this small a credit union might be your best bet. These are basically just banks that are set up to direct your wages toward your debtors, but they will also help to reduce the payments for you and in some cases even delete some of your creditors all together. If you do have severe debt problems, such as debts over $10,000, you may have to turn to bankruptcy to help you. You may also set up payment arrangements with your creditors. You can make an agreement between you and your creditors that will allow you to repay a percentage of the debt over a set period of time, which is usually around five years.

The advantage to doing this is that you will have more control over your assets, have fewer restrictions and you won't be categorized as bankrupt. This is excellent should you be running your own business. However, sometimes, filing for bankruptcy is all that you can do. In this case, it helps to know the exact process. That is what the next section will help you with.

The Process of Bankruptcy

If you are thinking of declaring yourself bankrupt, it is absolutely necessary that you get your own legal or financial advice from a lawyer or legal representative, a qualified accountant, or a reputable financial adviser. You can't go it alone and expect everything to work out. When you file for bankruptcy you have to represent by someone that is certified to stand on your behalf.

You will then have to file all necessary paperwork to ensure that your case is handled quickly. Your bankruptcy petition will look at your income and you debts. You will list them all. I would suggest that you get a copy of your report so that you can accurately record all of your debts and clear up any debts that were written by error. If you dispute the creditor's claim, you should try and reach a settlement before you file your bankruptcy claim. Trying to do so after the bankruptcy order is made will be difficult and extremely expensive. You will then have to take your bankruptcy claim to the courts.

Once the bankruptcy order has been made it will be noted on your credit report and stay there for a period of up to 7 years. This was just a brief account of how to go about filing for bankruptcy, as this is book about getting out from under bankruptcy's shadow.

Chapter 13 vs. Chapter 7 Bankruptcy

When someone files for bankruptcy under Chapter 13, their goal is to have the opportunity to repay some or all of the debts that they have acquired in their name. This is different from a Chapter 7 which uses asset liquidation to recover from the debt. Chapter 13 allows the debtor to use whatever income they may have in the future to pay off the creditors. I shouldn't have to state that filing Chapter 13 Bankruptcy is great for someone that actually has a steady income, and can afford to ask for payment adjustments, or reductions.

The United States Bankruptcy Code gives the debtor a time span of 5 years to pay off your debts. While the attorney who represents you will safeguard your interests, the entire process is carried out under the supervision of the courts. While debtors are allowed to keep all of their property that is considered an asset, the court has to pre-approve a new interest-free plan for repayment of the debt.

A written plan will be created that will outline all of the expected transactions, and the expected duration. The repayment must begin within thirty to forty-five days after the case has started. You will not have to deal with the transitory stage of having a middle man do the payment like you will get in Chapter 7 Bankruptcy. Although in some cases people may involve a trustee who would take care of paying out the money to the creditors if they want to. According to the law, the creditors must strictly stick to the repayment plan that is approved by the court and they can't collect any claims from the debtor personally.

Your attorney will prepare new repayment plan that best works for you. The one advantage of Chapter 13 over Chapter 7 Bankruptcy is the full discharge option that is not available in chapter 7. For example, if a debtor manages to complete all of their payments that are set up in the plan, he/she is given a full plan discharge. Also repayment can be created even if creditors disagree with it, as long as it is approved by the Court. To be eligible for chapter 13 bankruptcy, you must have a regular income. There are a few other items needed for filing a Chapter 13 Bankruptcy. Just ask your lawyer to explain them.

If filing for bankruptcy is an opportunity for a debtor to emerge out of a financial crisis and start afresh, then Chapter 7 of the Bankruptcy Code is the way to do it a bit quicker. Under Chapter 7 of the Bankruptcy Code all property that is considered to be non-exempt is sold and the proceeds are distributed to the creditors.

In most cases where Chapter 7 is brought into play there are no assets to lose so it really is quicker. This method is also called liquidation because you will turn your assets into cash. Chapter 7 Bankruptcy is the most common form of bankruptcy filing and makes up about 65% of all bankruptcy filings. Like I said it is one of the faster ways; especially if you don't have to get other asset owners involved. Chapter 7 lets you get rid of your debts in months of the attorney filing a bankruptcy petition as opposed to years that go with filing for Chapter 13.

This type of bankruptcy works by getting a trustee to collect all of your non-exempt property, sell the assets and distributes proceeds from this sale to appropriate creditors on your behalf and you don't have to pay them to do it. Most of the time this means that you will lose all your assets, so it is best to think before you do it. Under Chapter 7 Bankruptcy, the debtor receives a discharge on all dischargeable debts. Some of these debts are: child support, taxes and student loans that are discharged under Chapter 7 Bankruptcy. An added advantage with Chapter 7 bankruptcy is that by signing a reaffirmation agreement you can continue to pay for a car loan or a mortgage.

This agreement is in place because as per the US Government Bankruptcy Code a debtor could be allowed to retain some or all of his property. This is best for people who do not have a steady income coming in. To file you have to get a lawyer to represent you to the court and simply do as they advise you to. Be sure the information you provide is complete and correct.

CHAPTER 2- HOW TO GET OUT OF DEBT FAST

Getting into debt is easy; it is getting back out of debt that is hard. This section is going to try to give you alternatives to filing for bankruptcy. There are some steps that you should try before filing for bankruptcy. This section will show you the top ways to get out of debt before bankruptcy is necessary.

1)Take Advantage of your Assets

If you have assets that offer you some significant equity, such as a home or a car you may be able to use these as a way to deal with your debt. For example, you could get a loan on your home that is big enough to pay off your debts. You could be saving a great deal of money on interest if you pay off high interest credit card debt in return for lowering your debt cost. If you have a car, you should think of selling it, paying off your debts and buying a used car.

2)Increase your Income

Try getting another job and use the money from this job to only pay off your debts. You can make a list of your debts and interest rates. Pay off the debts with the highest rates first and work your way down. This may sound tedious, but sometimes it is necessary.

3)Put a hold on your credit cards

One of the best steps you can take to get out of debt is to stop adding to them. Credit cards are an amazingly easy way to add to your debts, as most of us don't see them for the problems that they are. I would suggest keeping only one card for emergencies, and throwing the rest of them away.

4)Set up a Repayment Plan

Cut back on your expenses as much as possible and try to use the extra cash for repaying your debts. Pay off the debts with the highest rates first and work your way down the list.

5)Consolidation Loan

A consolidation loan can seriously help you out of debt without declaring bankruptcy. This is when you get a loan to pay off all your debts and have just one payment to make. The new loan usually has a smaller repayment and a lower interest rate. If you can do this, you should.

6)Get a Credit Counselor

Be careful when you are thinking of using a credit counselor. Some of these so called credit counselors will just rip you off.

Powerful Lessons Someone Who Has Gone Bankrupt

There are basically 2 types of credit counselors out there to help you, and they are for profit and "nonprofit". They are both the same and do the same job and both charge a fee. Credit counselors can help you in teaching you how to get control of your debt. But I must warn you that many people do not fully understand all the ramifications involved in turning to them, such as:

- How it will affect your credit rating.
- The credit bureau will record that a plan is in place.
- Are your payments too high?

Your payments should be high enough helping you reduce your debt your debt but not so high that you have nothing left over. If you do not have money left over at the end of the month to pay for anything else you may find that you end up defaulting on your payments. Most people agree that your repayment term should be three to four years. It is a stipulation in the new Bankruptcy Reform Bills that the term be 3-5 years. Any time longer than this is proven to have a very high failure rate, because people cannot see their debts ever being gone and just skip it.

7)Informal Agreements- Timely Payment Agreement.

In some cases you can make a payment agreement with your creditors to set up a payment plan that will allow you to pay them back. This will help preserve your credit rating. This is a lot like getting a debt consolidation loan except you do not borrow the money to pay them off.

8)Informal Lump sum Agreement.

You may be able to pay less than 100 cents on the dollar if you choose to take this route. For example, you may be willing to pay a lump sum to the creditor of say 50% of the amount owed in order for the balance of the debt to be written off. This method is best if you have only a small amount of creditors.

9)Chapter 13 Bankruptcy

You are probably a good candidate for Chapter 13 bankruptcy if you are in any of the following situations:

a. You have a real and sincere desire to repay your debts, but you need the protection of the bankruptcy court to do so.

b. You are behind on your mortgage or car loan, and want to make up the missed payments over time. Chapter 7 bankruptcy doesn't let you do this. You can make up missed payments only in Chapter 13 bankruptcy.

c. You need help repaying your debts now, but want to be able to file for Chapter 7 bankruptcy in the future. This would be the case if for some reason you can't stop adding to the debt.

d. You are a family farmer who wants to pay off your debts, but you do not qualify for a Chapter 12 family farming bankruptcy because you have a large debt unrelated to farming.

e. You have valuable property that is not exempt. When you file for Chapter 7 bankruptcy, some of your property is exempt from collection. If you have a lot of nonexempt property, Chapter 13 bankruptcy may be the better option.

f. You received a Chapter 7 discharge within the previous six years.

g. You have someone who is in debt with you. If you file for Chapter 7 bankruptcy, your creditor will go after the co-debtor for payment should you not be able to pay. This happens should you get credit with a co-signer.

h. You have a tax debt. If a large part of your debt consists of federal taxes, what happens to your tax debts may determine which type of bankruptcy is best for you.

i. If all else fails, you will have to file for Bankruptcy

Can Debt Management Help Avoid Bankruptcy?

If you are in credit card debt, you should consider debt management to help avoid things like bankruptcy and help you clear your debts. Good credit card debt management should give you a realistic method to deal with your spiraling debts. You have probably already noticed that your creditor's high interest and late fees are making it impossible for you to manage your debts. You are in a serious mess, right?

The best way to resolve this is to switch to weekly payments. Paying your credit card debt weekly fits into most people's pay cycles and doesn't burden you with any surprises at the end of the month. They can also lower your total interest because some cards apply it on an hourly basis.

You should also confer with the Consumer Counseling Center of America, a non-profit group that assists anyone in serious financial predicaments like yourself. Credit counselors are available to assess your debts, create a resolution plan, and contact all your creditors to renegotiate your interest and monthly repayments. The CCCA can bring your account balances up to date, stop creditor calls, maintain current payments, and settle accounts in major arrears.

To take advantage of the many benefits the CCCA can offer you, you have to use self-discipline in relation to your finances. Start by stopping impulse buying. Counseling can only help if you cut or completely stop your credit card spending. You should either destroy your cards or have just one on hand in case of any emergencies. However, your remaining card must have a lower limit and interest.

Another method is to transfer all your existing credit card balances onto one low interest card. You will have to monitor all your balance transfers at the 0% interest level. This option can be very helpful in lowering interest payments. However, be cautious. Many people have been conned into believing that the companies could do what they claimed – eliminate credit card debt with just a nominally tiny charge. So many people have fallen victim to these witch doctors of credit repair. You must check into the background of any credit counselor you are considering.

The best person who can lower your debts is you. Using a workable budget, sticking to it, eliminating unnecessary spending, and sticking to essential purchases only will help you control and eventually get rid of all your debts.

Is it Wise to Consolidate Debt in One Monthly Payment?

Significant credit card debt is not unusual today with many individuals carrying credit card debt of $9,500 on average. With such balances and high interest rates ranging from 18-25%, debt management and debt consolidation services may be a good option if you ever want that debt to disappear. Debt consolidation can help you better manage your debt owed to several creditors by consolidating those bills into one single loan and, thus, one monthly payment. In addition, you will repay the debt at a lower interest rate.

Powerful Lessons Someone Who Has Gone Bankrupt
Debt management includes far more than bill consolidation services. Debt management includes a wide array of services such as credit repair, debt reduction, education and counseling, negotiation and other assistance. Debt consolidation to rid of bad credit is an excellent step toward repairing a negative credit reputation.

Debt consolidation is a very similar option in efforts to improve your debt situation. The consolidation company will negotiate with your creditors and make arrangements for you to repay the debt at a lower payoff amount and more quickly eliminate that debt. Consolidation is intended to help those consumers with debt as high as $5,000. You will repay the debt at a lower interest rate and with the convenience of one monthly payment.

Debt consolidation companies can help alleviate the burden of multiple monthly payments, yet many individuals hesitate to utilize consolidation services because of those who have been victimized by illegitimate consolidation companies. When choosing a consolidation company, you must do carefully. It is always a good idea to research the company's record, negative consumer reports or evidence of a poor reputation. There are many consolidation companies available today with no fee or, if anything, a small fee. The advantages of debt consolidation, though, outweigh any small fee associated with the services. Consider this as you choose the best company for you.

Once you find a good consolidation company to use, though, you can begin to reap the benefits of debt consolidation. Specifically, consolidation companies can help you reduce your high interest rates, waive late fees, lower your monthly payments, avoid bankruptcy and more quickly eliminate your debt. To help overcome high debt and a financial crisis, payoff your credit cards and outstanding debt at a lower interest rate with the help of debt consolidation.

The Difference between Debt Settlement and Consolidation

Debt settlement and debt consolidation is not the same thing. While they both help reduce your debt, they each affect your credit score and pocketbook differently. Before signing up with any debt management company, make sure you understand the pros and cons of their approach. And of course, be a smart shopper before signing any contract.

Debt Settlement – Instantly Eliminate Debt But at A Cost

A debt settlement company gets your creditors to wipe out part of your debt immediately. Creditors will reduce your debt because they become afraid that you will go into bankruptcy and you won't be able to pay them back the money you owe. With smaller payments, you can more easily wipe out your principal.

But with debt settlement, your credit will be in poor shape for a couple of years. Debt settlement is treated like a foreclosure or bankruptcy by lenders. So it will be difficult to get decent credit, at least for two years. You will also have a tax liability with the eliminated amount.

Debt Consolidation – A Slow Approach to Debt Relief

Debt consolidation companies handle your creditors and payments. You send them one payment, from which they pay your accounts. They also negotiate lower rates with your creditors, helping you to get out of debt sooner.

With this approach, your creditors will temporarily freeze access to new credit. They will want to see in the next year that you are making regular payments and reducing your debt. Your credit score may also drop, depending if your lenders report that you are working with a debt consolidation company. But after a year, you will be able to apply for new credit, possibly with prime rates.

Before you sign up any debt management company, make sure you research several companies before settling on one. Ask about their fees and process. Comparison shopping will give you a good idea on how reasonable the fees are. Details about the process will tell if the company is experienced in this type of debt management.

The sooner you reduce your debt, the faster you will improve your credit score and your finances. Debt management companies can help you get started.

CHAPTER 3- REBUILDING YOUR IDENTITY BY REBUILDING CREDIT

One of the best things about getting a fresh start on your credit by filing for bankruptcy is that it allows you a chance to rebuild your credit rating in the future. However, it is important that I tell you that your credit rating won't improve as long as all your old, negative information is still listed with credit reporting agencies, which as I said before can last for up to 5 years. All three major credit reporting agencies know all about you and your debts before you even filed for bankruptcy. This information includes late payments, charge-offs and judgments that were made against you. After your discharge, all these debts should be listed on your credit report as "Included in BK." If they are not listed that way, they appear to still be active accounts in collection status, which could severely change your chances to get credit. Unfortunately, creditors rarely report updates in credit records after a bankruptcy discharge.

A couple of months after your discharge, you should take the time to order credit reports so that you can make sure all your discharged debts are listed as being included in your bankruptcy. You can contact the three major credit reporting agencies for your accurate credit report. These are Trans Union, Equifax, and Experian. There are some more things that you can do to get your credit back in shape after bankruptcy; they are:

Give Yourself Credit:

The best way that you can rebuild your credit after a bankruptcy is to establish credit accounts that will report positive information on you. You will have to get a single credit card with a small credit limit, use it rarely and pay the entire balance every month before the due date. This doesn't work if you only pay minimum balances.

Read the Small Print:

After your discharge, you will likely get several offers for credit cards and other loans very quickly. You will need to know what you're getting into before you accept these offers. Make sure that you fully understand the interest rate, any other fees and the expected monthly payments before you open a new credit account. You have to think that credit card companies will offer anything to get you hooked, however many of the great offers are only introductory and will double your payments later on.

Prove Your Payments:

Even after your debts are discharged through bankruptcy, you may need proof that you don't owe these creditors before you can establish yourself again. Keep a couple of copies of your discharge papers from the court so that you can prove certain debts were discharged if you need to in the future. This will make your job much easier in the end.

Make all of your payment on time:

Most credit card companies and utilities report late payments to credit reporting agencies. If you make late payments every month, future creditors always see you as a bad credit risk. Also, you should note that most credit cards add a late fee whenever you're late with a payment, which only makes your payments higher. You will have to avoid paying late by paying your accounts in full on or before the due date.

Can a Debt Consolidation Loan Help Rebuild Your Credit?

If you've been in the process of working to develop a meaningful debt management program, you may be wondering what various options are available to you and you may be wondering what elements you will want included in an overall debt management plan. If you've found that your debt is becoming more and more out of control, the need for a debt consolidation program that works may have become imperative.

Through this article you will be provided with an overview of how a personal debt consolidation loan can be an important element of a comprehensive debt management program or debt management plan. Armed with this information you will be better able to determine whether or not a personal debt consolidation loan is the right choice for you and how you can make a personal debt consolidation loan a meaningful part of a comprehensive debt management program.

How a Personal Debt Consolidation Loan Works for You

A personal debt consolidation loan allows you the ability to combine all of your current debt into one loan. There are many solid benefits that are associated with a personal debt consolidation loan. For example, by combining all of your debts into one loan, you can enjoy significant convenience. Rather than having to pay multiple bills each month, you only have to make one payment.

You also save a great deal of money through a personal debt consolidation loan. You will no longer be plagued with higher interest rates, late fees and penalties when you obtain a personal debt consolidation loan. Indeed, over the course of the lifetime of the personal debt consolidation loan, you will realize a significant savings and put more money back into your pocket.

Elements of a Comprehensive Debt Management Plan

You need to keep in mind that a personal debt consolidation loan will not in and of itself resolve your financial problems for the long term. While a personal debt consolidation loan can be an important element in an overall debt management program, you need to include other elements as well.

First and foremost, in addition to a personal debt consolidation loan, if you want an effective debt management plan, you will want to make certain that you develop a meaningful and responsible budget. A budget must be a major component of any debt management plan if you really want to make progress in restoring order to your financial house ... not only today but into the future.

Second, unfortunately many people obtain a personal debt consolidation loan and then take off and accrue even more debt. It appears that these people feel that they have breathing room and can take on more debt.

The problem is that by obtaining a personal debt consolidation loan and then taking on more debt, you actually are making your financial situation far, far worse. You must be prudent with your debt and credit usage into the future or your personal debt consolidation loan really will serve no meaningful purpose at all.

Other Possible and Applicable Solutions to Credit Card Debt

Credit cards are accessories that once anyone has them, he is almost compelled to use them to pay off the expenses, without realizing that he can go into overdraft if he is not careful and keeps a regular track of the incidents happening in relation to the credit cards. It is therefore necessary for everyone to keep a close eye on how the events are unfolding around you in relation with your credit cards, because if you do not do that then there is a chance that you may find yourself in a tough situation.

People, who use overdraft facility that is provided by the banks for a long time and do not pay their required dues, can be subjected to following:

• They can be charged with heavy fines.

• There can also be heavy sanctions imposed on them.

• Their credit cards can also be held and destroyed

• They can also be categorized as people with bad credit history.

Keeping all these possible outcomes in mind, it is advisable to take the help of credit card debt management. Credit card debt management is a series of techniques that a credit card holder can use to get his credit card debts reduce and eventually eliminate his debts.

Credit Card Debt Management techniques that are available to any credit card holder are:

Debt negotiation – in this, what the borrowers need to do is try to negotiate a deal that could benefit both the holders and the main bank, which provides the credit cards. This technique will help both the parties in a win – win situation.

Debt management consultation – in this, what the borrowers are required to do is to go to a consultancy and try to find a way by which they can get out this situation of credit card debts.

A person with credit card debts can properly manage his credit card debts with all these credit card debt management techniques. All these techniques are available to all the people i.e. both the people with good as well as with bad credit history. So, people who have credit card debts, the advice would be to go for debt management rather than letting things go out of hands.

CHAPTER 4- USING BANKRUPTCY POSITIVELY

It may not seem like it, but bankruptcy can work for you if you want it to. Even though your bankruptcy will remain on your credit report, you can rest assured that you are not going to be marked for life. In fact, you will find that many companies will work with you even with a bankruptcy on your credit report. It is important to note however, that there will be some barriers to your getting back on your feet. Rebuilding your credit takes some effort and strategy on your part, but it is not impossible. You can turn the bankruptcy to your advantage. This section will show you how.

Deleting Credit Report Errors in 48 Hours

This is the absolute fastest way to correct any mistake that are made on your credit report and raise your credit score at the same time. However, you can't do this yourself. It can only be done through a mortgage company or a bank. If you apply for a bankruptcy home loan and find errors on your credit report, you can ask the loan officer to conduct a Rapid Rescore. However, you must be sure not to do this every time you apply for credit or you can find yourself in bigger problems.

The Rapid Rescore strategy will take some time however because it requires proper paperwork. For starters you will need proof that the item is incorrect. To do this, you will have to get the creditor to admit such on your behalf. For example, you can get a letter stating that the account is not your account, a letter stating the account was paid, a release of lien notice, a satisfaction of judgment, a bankruptcy discharge, a letter for deletion of collection account or anything else that will substantiate your claim. This is the same type of documentation that a bank or mortgage company would require from you for the credit accounts anyways. The difference is, now you can improve your credit score and receive a lower interest rate with it instead. The results are not guaranteed and will run you about $50 per account, so you should really be wary about taking advantage of it.

Deleting Bad Credit

This is the most area where you've heard of all the scams reported before. Credit repair clinics charge a huge fee for their services and promise you a clean credit report. Sometimes they even claim that they can give you a new credit profile! People are now spending hundreds, or even thousands, of dollars for something they can do themselves, which just ticks me off. Why? Most people don't realize that they can clear up their credit on their own. Removing your credit errors is simple. Deleting negative credit that is accurate requires some help.

Credit report mistakes easily disappear by using a simple dispute letter. It's that simple. If you have the paperwork proving that the error is real like I said above in Rapid Rescore, send copies of that along with the dispute letter. This will make the credit bureau's job easier and you will get your results quicker. If you don't have the documentation to prove that there are mistakes, you should send the dispute letter anyway. According to federal law; the credit bureaus have a reasonable amount of time to validate your claim. They will have to contact the creditor for verification of your dispute. From here the account will be reported properly or it will be deleted. It has been generally accepted that the reasonable amount of time is about 30 days.

Ride Someone Else's Credit Coat Tails

This is a fast and little known way to boost your credit score. But it requires a very trusting relationship. Basically, someone else will have to add you to their credit account for this to work. For example, when you are applying for a credit card, you may have seen the section to add a card holder. This is where you will want to add someone to your account because their payment history is now going to be reported on your credit report too. If they have perfect credit, now you will also have a perfect credit account. If you want to make this even better, use an aged account. What I mean by this is that if your friend or family member has a 10 year old credit card account with a perfect payment history and a balance of only half of the credit limit that means that this will become part of your credit history as well. The easy part about this is that this person just calls the credit card company and requests a form to add a cardholder. After this is done and the account is activated, their entire account history and future is now completely attached to your own. If you could secure 3-5 of these accounts; particularly if they are installment accounts your credit will reach the sky.

The hardest part of doing this is finding someone who has the good credit that will be willing to add you. Think about it; you already have a low credit score and bad credit, how eager do you think someone will be to make you a joint cardholder? Even your parents don't want you to damage their credit. Here's how you can get them, you do not need to possess the card, and you just need your name on it! In other words, the person who adds you could add you as a card holder and never give you the card or PIN or any information on it. Since the bills and all account information are still going to be sent to the person's address, you won't know anything about the account. Explaining this to people could give you many people who are willing to do it. And you still benefit with a higher credit score.

The Round Robin Plan

This strategy is one of the oldest credit building tricks you can pull. It used to be handled through secured savings accounts. But now, it's much easier to do because they have secured credit cards. In fact, I've used this method myself. Here's how it works: Take $1,000 (or whatever you can afford) and get a secured credit card. Once you get the card, get a cash advance of 70% of your credit limit. Now get a second secured credit card. Once you get this one, you will want to get a cash advance of 70% of your credit limit on this card. Use the money to get a third secured credit card. Once you get the card, get another cash advance of 70% of your credit limit.

Now that you are finished getting the cards, you will want to open a new checking account with the final cash advance. You will use this account only for making payments on your three new credit cards. If you make your payments on time every month, your credit score will get better because you now have three new perfect payment credit cards. It is important that I point out that at first, your credit score might drop a few points because of the fast, and multiple accounts being opened. However, if you wait for about 4 months and have no new accounts or any delinquencies of any account, you will see your credit score increase.

Pay on Time

This one is kind of obvious, but I cannot stress this any further. If you don't your credit score will decrease. This happens no matter how late your payment is. For some reason people still think that if they are only a few weeks late, it's all good. Well, for the loan company, if you pay late but consistent, they make a lot more money with late fees and more interest. For you, this means lower credit score. If you think in the long-term and credit score, you will see what I mean.

Pay down Your Debts

You have to remember that you're dealing with high-level statistics and probabilities which evaluate and forecasts trends in your paying behavior. You can never pay off your revolving debt completely. Think about it. Your credit score is a reflection of your ability to manage your credit. If you pay off your debt you are not managing your debt. If you maintain a balance of nothing, you have nothing to manage. It no longer exists. And you cannot manage what is not there. Therefore, when you are thinking in terms of credit score, you have demonstrated your ability to swiftly pay off accounts so that you can avoid managing them. Don't get me wrong; if you're over extended to begin with you will want to pay off what's necessary to make your credit profile look great. Then you need to manage the remaining credit. That is how you decrease your credit score. Creditors want to know that you can manage your credit account so you have to have a balance to do that.

Powerful Lessons Someone Who Has Gone Bankrupt
Don't Close Any Accounts

Even if you pay off continually revolving debts, do not close the account completely. The longer an account is open with no negative reports on it, the better it reflects in your overall credit score. This occurs because the creditors weigh in the averages in the credit score formula. Many credit experts will tell you to maintain a balance of 30% of your credit limit. However if you keep it at 70% you will still keep a healthy credit score

Don't get New Credit

You have to steer away from getting any new credit unless it is absolutely necessary. Every time you apply for credit, an inquiry is added to your report, and every inquiry that is made drops your credit score. When you have fresh credit, there is no track record how you will manage your credit account. Why risk the drop? You have to remember, your credit score is about risk assessment. You should get credit for your housing, transportation, college or continued education and 3-5 credit cards. That's really all you need anyway unless extravagant spending is what you're looking for. If you want more credit, request an increase on your current cards rather than apply for new ones.

Mix Credit Types

If you show creditors that you can handle different types of credit at the same time, you are rewarded with a great credit score. To do this, get installment loans for car, personal loan or mortgage. Get revolving credit as well like credit cards: Visa, MasterCard, Gas cards, department stores, etc. By mixing it up, you will be able to demonstrate that you can manage your credit because you will have short term and long term credit with a fixed payment plan in place. Keep these accounts open with a balance of 70% or less and be sure to pay them on time and watch your credit score soar.

Don't File For Bankruptcy or Foreclosure

Here's the most obvious advice: Don't file for bankruptcy or foreclosure if you can avoid it. These reports will stay on your credit report for 10 years and always decrease your credit score. If you are looking to quickly rebuild your credit history after a bankruptcy or foreclosure, I would recommend that you use the Round Robin strategy that I mentioned above and get secured credit cards. Now you can even get a car loan or mortgage right after bankruptcy.

CHAPTER 5- HOW TO RECOVER FROM BANKRUPTCY

Using Secured Credit Cards

For most of us, the thought of using secured credit cards doesn't seem that appealing. However, it is a great way to establish your credit rating after a bankruptcy. Like I stated in the previous section, the round robin strategy is perfect for this method of rebuilding your credit.

A secured credit card is basically just a term used to describe a credit card that you have prepaid. How it works is that you will get a credit card limit that is equal to the amount of money that you put in as a deposit. To the untrained eye, this is no more than paying cash + interest for goods and services. This doesn't seem like a good idea at first, but I will tell you it is a great way to raise your credit score. Secured credit cards were invented for this very reason.

As long as you maintain a 70% balance on your credit card and make all payments on time, you are good and this will entitle you to raise your credit limit and help you recover from bankruptcy in the long run. There are many different types of secured credit cards on the market right now and you have to be picky about which ones you should go for. So many banks and companies are offering them that they are competing with different incentives to get you to theirs. The most popular of them are:

CHASE PREPAID MASTERCARDS AND VISA

This prepaid credit card offers you 0% interest on your prepaid credit card which is great for helping you to keep those payments up. They require at least $500 dollars deposit, however you can pay more. I would recommend at least $1000. Chase cards are recognized and accepted everywhere that Visa and MasterCard are. Since they also offer unsecured cards, no one will know which version that you are using. This is good for the person that really doesn't want it obvious that they are using a prepaid card. Chase also runs off of their own banking institution, so when you have established your good standing with them, they may upgrade you to an unsecured card by transferring your balance and raising your credit limit later on. They will usually make a reference to your account after 6 months. Some other secured credit cards with a similar offer are:

• Orchard Bank MasterCards

• First Bank Visa

- Eufora prepaid MasterCard

- Centennial

- Premier Bank

CAPITAL ONE

The prepaid deal that you will get form Capital One is actually quite remarkable. You can make a deposit and get a higher credit limit than that of your deposit amount. This is rather excellent as they really give you a chance to work on your credit. Capital One does charge fees for cash up front as well as interest fees of up to 25%.

That is the big drawback here. You are also only allowed to take out 25% of the total limit on cash withdrawal all together so it makes the round robin approach to rebuilding credit impossible. It is a great card to have as far as the security deposit though and is worth considering. You can also get rewards cards when you apply for some of these cards. These cards can request as little as $200 for a deposit. You can still earn your credit back when you go through any of these and thousands of other offers. I would suggest however, that if you can, try to go through banks and financial institutions for your secured credit cards as these offer better turnaround times for re-establishing your credit.

Using Mortgage

A lot of people who go into deep debt promise themselves never to borrow again. Once they experience bankruptcy, they want to avoid going into debt like the plague. Credit scores are devastated by declaring bankruptcy and it is very easy to see why no one wants to go through it again. In case you haven't heard credit scores are the basically just the numerical way that your credit worthiness is identified to creditors. Your numbers will tell them what they need to know about you. If you don't understand the numbers I will break it down to you.

➢ 300 to 500 is very bad

➢ 500 to 600 is bad, but you can still get a mortgage or a very high rate auto loan with this score

➢ 600 to 700 is poor but again you can still get a mortgage with a reasonable down payment, or a high rate auto loan

➢ 700 to 800 is just OK

➢ 800 plus is good

Knowing this, you must know credit scores are not just used for borrowing. These numbers are sure to affect just about every aspect of your financial life in the future. Here are examples of the types of companies that use them to decide whether to do business with you AND they will also set your payment rates:

• Employers

• Auto, Life, and Health Insurance

• Apartment Rental

• Bank Accounts

• Utility companies are trying

So even if you don't want to your credit score to determine your life, you really need to use a mortgage to rebuild your credit scores.

Powerful Lessons Someone Who Has Gone Bankrupt

A mortgage may sound ridiculous as it is a major debt but it is really a great way to prove your worthiness. A mortgage is the quickest, easiest, safest, and best way to rebuild your scores. Let me show you how.

Quick – You can't do anything that will move your credit scores higher faster than a mortgage. The reason for this is because it is a larger debt and carries a lot of weight in your scores because of it.

Simple - Believe it or not getting a decent mortgage is much easier that getting a decent credit card or car loan. Pre-approval is a great way to go about it, so long as your bankruptcy has not been filed sooner than 6 months ago.

Safe - You are already paying rent for your house or apartment, so why not pay to own? It is a debt that you have to pay anyway, so why not make it work for you?

Makes sense - Mortgage lenders are considered by your scores as similar to a bank loan. They are not third rate lenders like the credit card, auto loans, personal loans that are always available to you. Third Rate Lenders have a negative effect on scores, but mortgages are looked at a real asset and getting one is a sure fire way to improve your score.

How to Refinance Your Mortgage

When you are ready to use mortgage refinancing as a way to get to the credit happy zone again after a bankruptcy, it can be hard to know if it is even the right thing for you to do. It can also be scary. For some people, doing this offers great financial benefits, and for others, it may never be worth it. You should think of using a refinancing mortgage offer after asking yourself these questions:

→How long do you plan to be in the house? Is it long enough to make refinancing the home worth it?

→How much higher the interest rate will be on your new loan thanks to your new found bad credit

→Whether or not you are already paying for private mortgage insurance

→How much the closing costs will be on the new loan

→Are there any extra fees and charges that will make the loan less affordable to pay back?

→The amount of equity that you have built up; does it make an equity refinance loan more approachable?

→Whether or not you plan to do cash-out refinancing later on

→Can you really afford it?

If you are wondering whether or not mortgage refinancing is a good idea after you have declared bankruptcy, I already stated that it is a great way to bring your credit back up and faster. Here are a few general mortgage refinancing tips that may help to make the process easier for you in the long run:

- If you do not plan on staying in the house very long, refinancing may not be the right thing to do

- Unless you are getting an interest rate that is easy for you to live with, refinancing your home may cost you more money in the long run than you can ever fully and comfortably deal with.

Powerful Lessons Someone Who Has Gone Bankrupt

- If you do take out a mortgage, you should keep an eye on rates; especially if they are offering variable ones as they will change on you. Bad credit refinancing does not offer you fixed rates.

- Choose a refinancing mortgage loan only if it going to help you. If you get in over your head, you will just end up back in bankruptcy or worse.

- If you are paying private insurance on your current mortgage, refinancing might help you to get rid of this extra expense.

- Closing costs when you have bankruptcy in your hands can be murder. If you plan on refinancing your home to help you get out of bankruptcy hell, be sure to remember how much the closing costs on the new loan will cost you and that you can live with it. When you are trying to take advantage of bankruptcy mortgage refinancing, the most important decisions you make will involve interest rates and the lender you choose to go through.

The interest rates alone are extremely hard on bad credit borrowers. The amount that you pay will greatly impact your monthly mortgage payment and the total amount of money that you will have to pay over the loan. The lower your interest rate, the better off you will be. Here is when the lender you choose will come into play. By using a lender who offers low interest rates, lending fees, closing costs, you can save a great deal of money and truly make your efforts to refinance worthwhile.

If you are looking for a little advice on finding low interest rates, the tips below will help:

• When you are refinancing after a bankruptcy, don't take the first offer that comes around. Take some time and research your choices. Make comparisons and seek reviews from borrowers like you.

- When you have bad credit, you have to find a lender who is willing to work with you and offer you reasonable loan terms.

- Know your credit score before you start looking as this will be the most beneficial to you. Try to get rid of all blemishes from your credit report before applying for a refinance. Like I said before, it is very important to getting approved.

Using Home Equity

In case if you have recently been through a bankruptcy it can be difficult to find the money that you need. The fact is that regardless of how hard you try, it seems that your bankruptcy is always standing in your way; at least for the next 7-10 years.

If this happens to you, you might want to consider looking into getting a bad credit home equity loan in order to help you rebuild your credit and get the money that you need. There are several advantages to using a bad credit equity loan to cover your financial needs, but it will be annoying. First of all, when you're looking at a bad credit home equity loan, it's important that you understand exactly what equity is.

Equity is basically the amount that you have actually paid toward your house or real estate, in comparison to the actual value of the property. You have to remember that you will not see a definitive number describing this but a percentage, and this is considered to be an indication of how much the house or property you actually own. The general rule here is that you will want to have as much equity built up as possible. After all, the more it's worth the better. A house that still has its full mortgage on it isn't going to be worth as much as the same house for the same price when the mortgage has been nearly paid off. I have to tell you that banks and other lenders look at this when they are considering granting a bad credit home equity loan, because the remaining portion of the mortgage will have to be paid with any money that is gained from selling the house should they need to foreclose on the property. When you are seeking a bad credit equity loan, the equity that you have built up in your house is generally considered to be completely separate from the actual house.

Loans that are taken out on equity are taken out on the house too, but the value of the equity is a much greater deciding factor than the value of the home on its own. Whether you believe it or not, a bad credit home equity loan really does offer many advantages. Perhaps the best one is that the generally high value of equity can help individuals who have recently filed for bankruptcy to get an interest rate that they might otherwise be unable to receive. These loans also tend to have a higher approval rate, more finance options, and the option to either take out a full loan or to create a line of credit instead.

The fact is that you can get credit again after bankruptcy. Bankruptcy is meant to give you a fresh financial start, and the ability to rebuild credit is part of that new start. Of course, like all good things; there is a process that you have to follow to rebuild credit after bankruptcy and it can be full of pitfalls. Some of these can be avoided.

•Don't take out loans or use credit unless you can afford to make the payments on time. That may sound obvious, but many good consumers make the mistake of taking out loans they can't afford to pay every day. Don't get so eager to rebuild your credit after bankruptcy that you feel you need to rush into it. You need to figure out whether or not you can afford the payments. If you assume that you can keep the payments every month, but can afford to miss a few after a while, you will never get your credit up and will likely end up back in debt and worse than before. You're going to need detailed information to take out a new loan.

•Check your budget. If you don't have one; create one before you even consider applying for new credit. With your budget figure out exactly how much the payment on the new account will be. You can also use a loan calculator which will do all of this for you.

•Compare the amount of the payment amount to your available income. Available income means reliable income that is not committed to another area of your budget. Don't base it on money you might have, work with the money you do have. Don't forget to leave some for savings/emergencies, so if this new loan payment means you're spending all of your monthly income, you can't afford it.

•Beware of hidden fees. There are many reputable lenders who specialize in offering second chance loans, but they will have a higher interest rate. This is offered to consumers who have low credit scores or have filed bankruptcy. But not all lenders who will do this are reputable. When you've filed bankruptcy and know that your credit options are limited, you may be tempted to accept terms that would normally ridiculous. Lenders know this and some will take advantage of post-bankruptcy clients by giving them unnecessary fees, crippling late-payment charges, and hidden costs. It's more important that you watch out for this after bankruptcy.

•Find out exactly what fees and costs are associated with the account. Don't be lulled into a false sense of security by terms like, "No up-front costs." Many credit cards that target post-bankruptcy and low-scoring consumers add these "processing charges" and "annual fees" directly to your account—which means that you may receive a credit card with a $250 credit limit and $175 or more in charges already made to the account. Know the penalties for late payments and going over your credit limit. Often, one late payment can send an account like this spiraling out of control. You miss a $50 minimum payment, and then a $35 late charge is added. Because your new credit limit is low, the late charge puts you over your credit limit, triggering another $35 charge—which, of course, puts you further over your credit limit. By the time your next statement rolls around, your $50 minimum payment has turned into a request for $150 or more to "bring your account current." And if you aren't able to make that payment, it just keeps growing. For many post-bankruptcy consumers, that scenario is all too familiar.

There's no room for that kind of error when you're trying to rebuild after bankruptcy, so be very certain that you know what kind of charges may apply and what circumstances might trigger them. Read the entire agreement carefully. It's true that most people don't read the fine print in all of their contracts, but it's a gamble—and it's all the more dangerous when you're dealing with the high-risk lenders. Remember that companies making loans to low-credit-scoring and post-bankruptcy consumers are taking a chance—and they're not going to take that chance without a significant payoff. Read and understand the entire agreement, and if you don't understand something, ask questions until you do.

Watch out for these common "predatory" practices: People who have filed for bankruptcy are often targeted by predatory lenders, because those lenders know that post-bankruptcy borrowers have fewer options, and that they may be so relieved to discover that they've qualified for a loan after bankruptcy that they won't be inclined to ask too many questions. Many consumers accept that because they think accepting extortionist terms is the only way that they'll qualify for credit after bankruptcy. It's not true. Hold out for a reputable post-bankruptcy lender.

You should also watch out for the predatory lenders that will try and get you with the bait and switch method. This is when a lender will reel you in by promising you one set of terms and then change them on you after you have agreed. The contract will state a variable interest rate. This means that they can change it whenever they want to. Be aware of this trick and look for it.

Another common trick is called loan packing. This is when your lender tried to get you in by insisting or even demanding that you add on a bunch of other services to your loan like insurance. This is not a forcible add-on and if they try to tell you it is, they are lying. Take your business somewhere else. Equity stripping is another trick that is used by lenders. How this works is that they will try to convince you to add extra items or services and they will try to get you to borrow against the loan which will lower your equity. Loan flipping is another tactic lenders will use. They will try to get you to repeatedly refinance your home equity which in turn strips your home's equity. They can even charge you more fees for doing it, so beware.

Only take out loans that you want and nothing else. Don't let them try to change your mind. The fresh start you gained in bankruptcy can be exactly what you need to get your financial life back on track and establish strong credit. Don't let unscrupulous lenders or over-eagerness push you to do something that you are not comfortable with. Remember to read the fine print in all written documentation.

Finding an Equity Lender to Trust You

Finding a lender for a bad credit home equity loan often requires you to take a little time to shop around and compare quotes before you can find one that you are comfortable with. If were you, I would search online as you can make comparisons.

Online lenders are often consulted for equity loans, since they can usually offer a lower interest rate than many walk in lenders. However, it's important that you take the time to compare the different loan offers and choose the one that's best for you and your needs as not all online lenders are the same. Some are better than others. Just check their reputation before signing up. You can't deny that a bad credit equity loan makes home equity loans one of the best ways to establish better credit. As a matter of fact with a 100% financing, you can easily tap into your home's equity, which is great if your home is more valuable now than when you bought it.

The fact is that you can borrow as much money against your home as its value is. On the other side your home's value is determined by a third party assessment that is also based on the selling prices of the homes that are listed around yours. I should note that you can use your equity to borrow in one lump sum payment with a home equity loan or you can take it as you need it with a line of credit. Believe it or not, home equity loans really do have the lower rates, but lines of credit are far more flexible.

This dot com era has steadily risen and you can't deny that online lenders offer better loans because they have to compete with companies from all over the nation. Not to mention financing companies also have lower overhead costs when they are online and this allows them to pass on greater savings to you. It is worth pointing out that with so many prime lenders to choose from, it is easy to get very overwhelmed trying to find one to stick with.

It is very important that you base your loan search solely on the money that you have to pay. You should also as that you get a no obligation loan quotes to compare rates and fees. With most home equity loans, fees will come up like annual processing or minimum balance fees. These are more likely to be a part of the terms. Since these can add hundreds of dollars to your loan costs, it is quite important that you check the fine print extremely carefully. After you have chosen your lender, the application process is simple. As a matter of fact, most of them will allow you to apply online and you can get your answer within minutes or days. It is a very simple thing to do that can help you rebuild your credit after bankruptcy very easily.

CHAPTER 6- ERASING DAMAGES TO CREDIT BECOMES CHILD'S PLAY

Basically, you can't erase the past. Negative records that you can mount up, such as bankruptcy and collection accounts will remain on your credit report for 7-10 years. And there is nothing that you can do about it, however; with some time and little bit of effort, you can improve your credit even before these bad records legally expire. Here are five easy steps you can take to rebuild your credit while it is still in default.

Step 1: Check out the damages

The first step that you have to take in rebuilding your credit is to look at exactly where you stand. This is an important step to take, which is why I have written it more than once. Your report can change every week, so checking it often is necessary. Here is where you have to just take it and order all three of your credit reports and all three of your credit scores. You can easily get your credit report online, and it is secure. By the way, no matter what you think checking your own credit data never damages your credit scores. You will want to print each report and review it very closely. Highlight any negative records or errors that are damaging your credit score. You will also want to make sure that you fully understand what your credit report says. If you don't understand it, how can you expect to correct it?

Step 2: Check the expiration dates

By law, any of the negative records that you garner must remain on your credit report for 7-10 years. The exact expiration date is going to vary; depending upon the type of record that it is. Paying off an old collection debt or discharging your bankruptcy does not get rid of these records; contrary to what most people believe. For each of the negative records that you will see on your credit report (including judgments, liens, charge-offs, late payments, bankruptcy filings, and collection records), you will have to look up and know the exact date that they are set to expire from your credit report. The reason for this is because you will then know when you can expect to see a major improvement in your credit score.

Step 3: Dispute the errors

I can't stress this enough! (Can you tell?) If you find anything at all that seems wrong to you; if you find any fraudulent accounts, or records that should have expired on you credit reports, you have the right to dispute these errors. To do this, you will need to send a separate dispute letter to each of the credit bureaus that are holding your account to correct your Equifax, Experian, and

TransUnion records. Once your dispute is received by the collection agency, the credit bureaus have 30 days to investigate and determine whether or not to make the change you have requested. Do not try to dispute anything that is accurate. Accurate information cannot be removed from your credit reports and it is a waste of time to attempt to dispute these records because it will not help you. Disputing positive information may actually harm your credit scores and cause you to garner fraud charges.

Step 4: Keep track of the positive

Just like how you need to discharge inaccuracies, you should also report anything positive. Since there is no way to remove negative information from your credit report, the best way to improve your score is to add as much new information as you can that is good. How to do this is to open up a new credit card account like I stated in the round robin approach in an above section. However, it doesn't stop there. You should also sign up for an online banking service that will let you keep a close eye on your accounts that you can print and dispute should you have to. Online banking is a sure fire way to keep a really good hold on information. You can also use online banking as a way to make instant payments to your creditors by adding them to your automatic payment plans. This will ensure that all of your payments are on time.

Step 5: Monitor your progress

It's easy to keep track of your credit score improvement because we now have a great deal of software that can do it for you. Instead of just giving you occasional access to your credit report and general email alerts, these new credit monitoring programs will give you things like access to your credit reports and credit scores, identity theft and fraud, credit score monitoring, daily alerts, and more. You can also choose to go through an online credit monitoring service which will send you your information in your email inbox every day.

Once you have signed up for a credit monitoring service, you will be able to track your credit score progress closely. Your credit score should improve regularly as you continue to use your credit responsibly and add new positive information to your credit reports on your own.

Should You Hire Professional Credit Monitoring Services?

To be able to use the credit monitoring service that I recommended above, it helps if you fully understand them. Credit report monitoring can be used after bankruptcy to help you as part of identity theft prevention and detection strategy. Although monitoring your credit report may not prevent many of the credit problems that we often find ourselves in, it can keep you up to date with anything that is going awry.

After you filed for bankruptcy, you will want to know exactly what is going on with your credit report if you want to keep it that way. You should understand however, that there are a variety of ways that a credit monitoring service is the best way for you to keep records of your credit report and scoring information. In the era of online identity fraud, you will need this more than ever. Nothing will undermine your efforts to recover from bankruptcy faster than having your identity stolen.

This section will focus on the things that you should know about credit monitoring services, so that if you are considering using one, you can make an informed choice. You will find many advertisements for credit monitoring services online and off that will make you think that they monitor your credit report so that at the precise moment an identity thief is at work, alarms are sounded, the thief is stopped immediately and you are fully aware of it. Although this is really why these services exist, the way that they really work is not as spectacular. The general purpose of credit monitoring services can really be explained in these basic points:

Early Activity Detection: The basic benefit and purpose of credit monitoring services is that they help you to quickly detect any unauthorized activity that takes place in your name. As I stated earlier, the victims often have 6 months of activity recorded in their name before they even know about it. Therefore, early detection can save you thousands of dollars in the long run.

It is Convenient: you should know that most of the services that a credit monitoring service provides can actually be done by you. However, hiring a monitoring service to do the work for you frees up much of your time and is extremely accurate.

What these Services Monitor: Although you can pay for many different levels of service, most of the time, these services will monitor the following:

Credit File Inquiries: The service will keep track of who is inquiring on your credit file and why. This information can be useful in detecting unauthorized activities.

New account activity. These days, a lot of people are learning that it is very common to find that someone has opened up a new account in their name. The service will monitor any new accounts that are opened in your name and report it to you. This will help you in recovering from bankruptcy as you can know exactly when someone makes a query in your name; which will prevent credit score decreases as every query lessens your score.

Address Changes. You can use this service to ensure that no one has changed your address which happens when identity thieves are applying for credit so that they can get credit cards etc. sent to them.

Collection Accounts. Unfortunately, many victims realize that they there identity has been stolen when they apply for and can't get credit. Your monitoring service will alert you to this.

Changes to account information. The service will monitor any changes to account and inform of them, such as if you refinance a mortgage.

Credit limit increases. When someone steals your identification, they will raise your credit limit so as to take advantage of it. You will be notified of this too.

Changes to public records. The service will monitor any changes to public records that would include bankruptcies

Changes to all existing accounts. You will be notified if your accounts become delinquent.

Account Closures. Any accounts that have been recently closed will be flagged and reported to you. Now that we know what the credit monitoring services actually follow, you need to know what to look for in a monitoring service, which are:

Source. The monitoring services will have to use a credit reporting agency to monitor your credit report. However, depending on the service, the information may be obtained from just one or all three major reporting agencies. For this reason, you will want to purchase a service or plan that monitors all three credit reporting agencies.

Frequency. When looking for a monitoring service how often they check is something that you should consider. Daily or weekly is best. Services vary, providing daily, weekly or monthly monitoring. As you would expect how often they monitor your credit report the better for you.

Credit updates. Some services will also provide periodic credit updates. This is a lot different from the alerts because the alerts only deal in changes. A periodic credit update will add the information in your credit accounts that have not changed.

Credit reports. These monitoring programs will always offer you a copy of your credit report. How often you will get one will vary depending on the service. Some services provide unlimited access to your credit file which means that you can check whenever you want to, while others provide a credit report quarterly. I would suggest that you get one that offers you unlimited access because should you choose to follow any of my advice about rebounding off bankruptcy, you will need a copy on hand.

Identity theft insurance. Some services will offer identity theft insurance as part of the package. Just be sure to read the fine print first.

Cost. Cost is obviously something that you should consider when choosing a monitoring service. Costs range from $39 per year for a very basic and one bureau monitoring service, to $200 per year for a premium and 3 bureau monitoring service.

When you are trying to recover from bankruptcy, keeping track of all of your credit accounts can be a life saver in keeping you on track. Of course, there is some stuff that a credit monitoring doesn't do, such as take the action for you. Trust me preventing Identity theft in this day and age is necessary in recovering from bankruptcy as it can save you from having illegal attempts made on your account which could put you right back where you started.

CHAPTER 7- HOW TO PROTECT YOURSELF FROM IDENTITY THEFT

This section is necessary if you want to recover from bankruptcy. A credit monitoring service can help with this. However there are other things that can help you in your fight. When you have declared bankruptcy, you do it to get a second chance. This can't happen if your identity is stolen from you. This will be a larger section as it covers a big aspect of keeping your credit on track. The crime of identity theft is on the rise big time. Recent surveys show there are currently about 9 million victims each year. How it works is that criminals steal Social Security numbers, driver's licenses, credit card numbers, ATM cards, calling cards, and anything else they can get their hands on that offers your information. They use this information so that they can impersonate their victims, spending as much money as they can in as short a time as possible before moving on to someone else. Right now there are two basic types of identity theft which are:

Account takeover: this happens when a thief gets a hold of your current credit account information and purchases products and services by using the actual credit card or just the account number and expiration date, and back of card code.

Application fraud: this is also called "true name fraud." The thief will use your SSN and other ID information to open new accounts in your name. This takes a lot of time to hear about unless you have a credit monitoring system working for you.

Generally, victims of credit card fraud are not liable for more than the first $50 of the loss (Lending Act, Fair Credit Billing Act, 15 USC sec. 1601). Most of the time, the victim will not be required to pay any part of the loss; however debit card users have less protection against fraud. When this fraud happens; your accounts will be wiped out, but you could be liable for the total amount of the loss depending on how quickly it is reported (Electronic Funds Transfer Act, 15 USC sec.1693). Even though most victims are usually not stuck paying their imposters' bills, they are often left with a bad credit report which can be horrible if you just went through a bankruptcy.

Meanwhile, you will difficulty getting credit, obtaining loans, renting apartments, and even getting hired at a new job. In fact, you can't take advantage of all of these efforts to help you learn to rebuild your credit when a fraud takes place.

Do you see now why this section is so important? Victims of identity theft find that the police can't do much to help you either, as it can be hard to prove that the fraud took place. Stealing wallets used to be the best way identity thieves obtained Social Security numbers (SSNs), driver's licenses, credit card numbers and other pieces of identification. Now they have many ways of getting your information without you knowing about it at all. Here is how:

Powerful Lessons Someone Who Has Gone Bankrupt

-       "Dumpster diving" in trash bins is common. Thieves look for whole credit card and loan applications and anything else that would contain SSNs.

- Stealing mail from mailboxes which can give them access to brand new credit cards, bank and credit card statements, pre-approved credit offers, investment reports, insurance statements, and even tax information.

- Accessing your credit report is easily done if the thief is an employer, loan officer, or landlord.

- They can get names and SSNs from personnel or customer files in the workplace.

- Shoulder snatching at ATM machines, direct debit purchases and phone booths is an easy way to get your pin numbers.

- Internet sources, such as via public records sites and fee-based information broker sites.

- Sending emails from your banks that asks you to visit a web site that looks like the banks in order to confirm account information. They call this phishing and it gets more popular every day.

You can't prevent identity theft in every case as identity theft is relatively easy because of lax credit industry practices, careless information-handling practices in the workplace, and the simplicity that goes with getting SSNs. But you can reduce your risk of fraud by following the tips in this section. The most important advice I can give you is to check your credit report at least once a year. You can catch the fraud quicker this way. Here are some more tips to help you.

Credit cards, debit cards, and credit reports:

1. You have to lower the number of credit and debit cards you carry around every day in your wallet. I would recommend that you do not use debit cards at all because of the potential for shoulder snatching anyway. Instead, you should carry one or two credit cards and your ATM card in your wallet and that is it. Debit cards may be popular but you have to take advantage of online access to your bank account to monitor account activity frequently. Report anything strange quickly.

2. When you are using your credit and debit cards at restaurants and stores, pay close attention to how the magnetic stripe information is taken. Dishonest employees have been known to use small hand-held devices which are called skimmers to quickly swipe the card and then they download the account number data onto a personal computer later on.

3. Do not use debit cards when you are shopping online. Use a credit card because you are better protected in case of fraud.

4. Photocopy of all your credit cards, debit cards, bank accounts, and other financial information such as the account numbers, expiration dates. Just don't carry it around with you in your wallet or purse. This way if the information is stolen, you can report it.

5. Never give out your SSN, credit or debit card number or other personal information over the phone, by mail, or on the Internet or if you are the one that initiated the telephone call.

6. Always take credit card receipts with you whenever you get one. Never toss them in a public trash container. Remember also not to carry them in the shopping bag.

7. Never allow your credit card number to be written onto your checks.

8. Watch the mail when you expect a new credit card to arrive.

9. Order your credit report at least once a year.

10. Get a free credit report from Equifax, TransUnion, and Experian

11. If your state allows it freeze your credit reports. By freezing your credit reports, you can prevent credit issuers from accessing your credit files except when you give your express permission. In most states, security freezes are available for free.

12. Several companies offer credit monitoring services for an annual fee ranging from $50-$120 a year like I said above, take advantage.

13. There are many identity theft insurance products that you can use. I don't recommend them unless they are free or a cheap add-on to an existing insurance policy.

14. When you are dealing with passwords and PINs, do not use the last four digits of your Social Security number, birth date, middle name, consecutive numbers or anything else that could easily be found out by thieves. You should think to use passwords that combine both letters and numbers.

15. Ask your financial institutions to add extra security protection to your account. Most will let you use more than one when accessing your account. Again, don't use easy things to figure out. If you are asked to create a reminder question, do not use one that is easily answered by others.

16. Memorize all your passwords. Do not write them down.

17. Cover your hand when you are using an ATM machine or debit.

18. Protect your Social Security number at all costs. Only give it out when it is absolutely necessary. It is this information that the thieves are looking for. If a business asks you for your SSN, you should ask if there is an alternative number that can be used instead. Ask to see the company's written policy on SSNs.

19. Do not have your SSN or driver's license number placed on your checks. This may sound like a given, but you would be surprised how many people do this.

20. Do not say your SSN out loud in public. Don't let anyone say it out loud either

21. Examine your Social Security Personal Earnings and Benefits Estimate Statement each year.

22. Do not carry your SSN card in your wallet unless you know that you will need it. Photocopy your cards instead and then make them wallet size.

23. If you live in a state that uses the SSN as your driver's license number, I would tell you to simply ask for a different number.

24. Use a firewall on your home computer which will help to keep hackers from getting hold of your personal identifying and financial data from your hard drive. This is especially important if you are using DSL or cable modem.

25. Install and update virus protection software to prevent a worm or virus from causing your computer to send out files.

26. Password-protect any of your files that contain personal information like, such as banking information and credit card info.

27. When shopping online, do business with companies that provide transaction security protection such as Verisign and read their privacy policies.

28. Before you get rid of your computer, use a wipe out utility program. Delete is just not good enough.

29. Never respond to email messages asking for your personal information, no matter who they are from. Your bank will not ask and if they do call them instead.

30. be aware that file-sharing and file-swapping programs like Ares, Morpheus, and Kazaa.

31. Never carry extra credit cards, debit cards, your Social Security card, birth certificate or passport in your wallet or purse.

32. If possible, do not carry other cards in your wallet that contain the Social Security number (SSN), except on days when you need them.

33. If you want to lower the amount of personal information that out in cyber space you can do these things: -Take your name off of marketing lists of the three credit reporting bureaus which are Equifax, Experian, and TransUnion; -Sign up for the Federal Trade Commission's National Do Not Call Registry; -Sign up for the Direct Marketing Association's Mail Preference Service. -Have your name and address removed from the phone book and reverse directories.

34. Install a mailbox that you can lock at your house. Or use a post office box or a commercial mailbox service.

35. When you are ordering new checks, pick them up at the bank. Don't have them mailed to your home.

36. When you pay bills, never leave the envelopes that have your checks or money orders in them at your mailbox for the postal carrier to pick up.

37. Each month, you will want to review your credit card, bank and phone statements

38. Try to make as many of your bill payments through automatic deductions from your checking account or use internet banking and pay them yourself.

39. Do not throw out pre-approved credit offers without tearing them up.

40. Use a gel pen for writing your checks because it has been stated that gel ink contains tiny particles of color that are trapped in the paper, so it is very difficult to wash the check and re-write it.

41. You must demand that financial institutions keep your data safe. Don't let your bank use easy to decode numbers on your cards. If you have been given the last four SSN digits as a default PIN, change it to something else immediately. Insist they destroy paper and magnetic records before getting rid of them.

42. When you fill out loan or credit applications, ask how the company disposes of them. Some auto dealerships, department stores, car rental agencies, and video stores have been known to be careless with customer applications once they are finished with

them. When you pay by credit card, ask the business how it stores and disposes of the forms. When you do this online, be sure the company uses secure transmission and storage methods.

43. Store all of your canceled checks in a safe place. If you rent a storage locker, take extra precautions when you are storing cancelled checks, tax return information, and other sensitive financial information. Thieves love these.

44. Store all of your personal information in your home, especially if you have roommates.

45. Any company that handles personal information should train all its employees, from top to bottom, on responsible information-handling practices.

CHAPTER 8- DON'T FALL VICTIM TO CREDIT REPAIR SCAM

With so many people who are looking for credit help after they have been forced to declare bankruptcy, there are many more people who are willing to capitalize off of them. You can find literally thousands of different advertisements online and elsewhere that promise you credit repair and not all of them are legal. Here are the most common:

SCAM #1 Getting a New Social Security Number

Many people are only allowed to have one Social Security number. It is against the law to use a different Social Security number to create a false identity. However, many criminals will offer this service to you for a fee. The thing is that since it is illegal, you are in for quite a bit of trouble. Not to mention, nobody ever seemed to wonder just where these SSNs come from. It is most likely that you are paying for a stolen identity. It is a perfect scam in that the thieves get the money for the transaction, and you will be the person that gets caught for scamming the SSN. It is quite brilliant, but many people fall for it. Even if they claim that this transaction is completely legal; IT IS NOT!!!!

SCAM #2 Getting a Federal Employer Identification Number (abbreviated as EIN or FEIN)

This is basically nothing more than a file segregation scam. For this scam, the criminals claim that you can obtain a federal tax ID number, as if you are a business, and end up with a clean credit record that is listed under that tax ID number. It is against the law to use an EIN to set up a false identity as well. Let me also tell you that a new credit report under an EIN will not even show a credit history. It is unlikely that a creditor would regard a new business with no credit history as a good credit risk. So it is also a waste of time.

SCAM #3 Challenging Everything Bad on a Credit Report

As I stated before, this is simply stupid. All credit agencies have to keep accurate records of negative entries on your credit history for up to seven years, and to keep records of any bankruptcies for as much as years. Sometimes truthful negative information may be reported beyond those time periods, but it is rare. You can't report false negatives on your credit report without suffering some consequences. If you are caught filing false claims, you could be in much trouble. I will say that this is a brilliant tactic though, and basically hard to prove a negative report claim knowingly took place.

SCAM #4 Clean Credit Scam

They claim that they clean your credit fast and use their contacts to get you a mortgage (or credit card or loan). This is one of the more recent credit repair scams and coincidentally it is also one of the most expensive. Con artists dangle the promise of needed money or loans in front of desperate consumers as an incentive for the consumer to pay them up front fees that never seem to end. Some of them actually claim to legit credit counseling agencies, while others imitate mortgage companies. And since there are genuine community nonprofit groups that really will help to teach the consumer and help them to find affordable mortgage loans, scammers may also try to imitate this. Any reputable community-based organizations will tend to focus on education, and they don't charge pikes of money to do it. They also work with lenders and government agencies you should have already heard of and are able to prove it.

SCAM #5 The 900-number for details on how to fix your credit.

This is a pitiful scam but it is still effective, and is often combined with any of the others mentioned above. While you are looking for help, the con artists are looking to keep you on the line as long as possible and make money from the per minute charges. It is just like every other 900 number scams. However this one is also easy to spot and work through. Scammers are often vague on details when they are talking to you on the phone. If you have trouble defining, understanding or explaining their proposed plan for cleaning your credit, that is a clue that it is a scam. You should also watch out for any offer of guaranteed credit with these numbers as it is almost certainly to be a fraud.

This is the same thing with anyone who claims quick fixes. You should really be on the lookout for nameless, faceless so called credit repair companies. Legitimate counselors will usually want a face-to-face meeting to go over all your financial details with you and they will also spend a great deal of time in trying to educate you on the process and how it really works. Here are some important questions that you need to ask, if you want to be sure that you are not dealing with a scammer:

- Who is coming up with the plan, and who can I speak to about it?

- Has this company had any problems before? You can find out by calling your state's regulatory or consumer offices to see if there are any complaints or actions being taken against them. Don't forget to check with the company's home state if you have to, and to run the business and names of the company's main executives through a couple of search engines.

- How are they paid, how much and when do they get their payment? Since you can do your own credit repair for free, this is why you should ask. It may be more beneficial to do it yourself. You should want to go with an organization that is affiliated with the two main nonprofits, the National Foundation for Credit Counseling and the Association of Independent Consumer Credit Counseling Agencies. They will help you for a small fee that is nowhere near the hundreds.

- What's the downside of this plan, if any? Any real credit counselors are careful to present the positives and negatives behind any plan. When they are scamming you, they will ignore the bad side and focus on the upside.

- Did you contact them or did they contact you?

- Why aren't you doing it for yourself? I should also note that you should not be told to make payments for your credit report. You're entitled to receive a free copy of each of your credit reports every year. Watch out for sites and services that are trying to charge you for it, or for those who try to charge you for your credit report when you opt for their credit monitoring service. Your credit report will not change no matter what is claimed and many scammers will tell you that you are to pay for the entire report but can get a portion of it for free. The fact that many say this is disturbing, but it happens every day.

The Most Common Lie Credit Repair Companies Tell You

If you have declared bankruptcy, you can't get credit for ten years. This is a common lie that credit repair companies will tell you. The truth is you can start building a positive credit history as soon as your bankruptcy is discharged. While creditors will be cautious in dealing with you at first, you can slowly show your fiscal responsibility, and build a solid history that can lead lenders to view you as a good credit risk long before the bankruptcy is off of your history report.

Stay Away from Bad Credit Repair Companies That Lie

As much as we want to believe that credit repair companies want to help out the underdog, many of them are unscrupulous on how they deal with them. They will lie and charge ridiculous fees and even outright fraud. Fortunately there are warning signs that you can see beforehand and recognize them. They are as follows:

➢ Do not use any credit repair company that doesn't follow industry standards or regulations to the letter. To find out, go to your own state government website and check.

➢ Do not use a credit repair company that claims to be able to completely wipe out or get rid of your bankruptcy; to remove accurate negative information from your credit history, or if they claim to be able to obtain credit for you no matter what your credit history states.

➢ Do not use a credit repair company that promises to utilize some sort of secret or little known holes in the system as a way to help you to remove information from your credit history.

➢ Do not use a credit repair company unless it easily gives you a written disclosure of your rights in relation to your credit history before they ask you to sign a contract. Any contract that you sign has to include all the terms and conditions of payment, a completely detailed description of the services they are giving you, including any guarantees of performance and an estimate of how long it will take for the contract to be completed. The agreement should also include a right to cancel the contract for at least three days, in case you have second thoughts.

➤ Do not use a credit repair company that tries to charge money before it has actually done anything to fix your credit.

➤ Do not use a credit repair company that tries to keep you from directly contacting the major credit bureaus on your own.

ABOUT THE AUTHOR

Wendy Turner is an entrepreneur whose early years as a business owner were marred with controversies resulting in bankruptcy. During her darkest financial moments, Wendy realized so many things about bankruptcy that she believes should be shared to everyone and be part of common knowledge.

Today, Wendy has successfully re-established her business and her value is now worth more than a million dollars.

www.ingramcontent.com/pod-product-compliance
Lightning Source LLC
Chambersburg PA
CBHW071306170526
45165CB00003B/1441